Years ago, I was sitting in a restaurant having dinner with my friend Barb, and we were discussing what we wanted out of life and WHEN we were going to do it. Barb had the ability to ask the deepest questions, she was incredibly curious and didn't tolerate excuses. She would challenge me and ask, "When are you going to do it"? Our mantra became "Some Day Is NOW".

Thank you, Barb for pushing me to take action, to stretch, to feel the fear and do it anyways. Thank you for believing in me and loving me.

Some Day is NOW!

Why Journal?

Awareness…. Writing is a powerful tool to help you create what you want and dump what you don't. Whatever you put in motion, stays in motion, whatever is at rest stays at rest (Newton's Law).

Our thoughts create our outcomes. Studies show that we think between 30,000 – 55,000 thoughts a day (most are unconscious) and approximately 85% of our thoughts are negative. Yet our unconscious thoughts are what are driving our outcomes. What if you could ON PURPOSE create the life you want? Awareness is key… you must know what you want, to get it. You must know what you're thinking to understand "why" you're where you are.

Journaling is an excellent tool to help you create awareness, to be intentional, to create the outcomes you want, to find solutions to where you are and to dump the stuff that is keeping you stuck.

The way you write takes on your own personality. There is no right or wrong way to do this. Some people need structure, where other people need complete freedom. This journal book as a blend; questions to create the structure and a blank space for you to think outside the box. Today is the first day of your life… you have a blank page before you. You are the author of your life. Will you create your day or let your day create you?

Some Day is NOW!

How this journal book works:

The first few pages are designed to get you to think about what you want, where you are and where you're going. *"Vision without action is merely a dream. Action without vision just passes the time. Vision WITH Action can change the world." ~Joel A. Barker*

You will create a focus at the beginning of this book of what do you want to be, do and have after you complete this journal plan. The book is set up as a three-month guide. Each month you will "check in" to see how you're doing on your overall goals. This isn't meant to stress you out. If you get off track, shake it off and start again. One of my favorite sayings is "So what, now what". You can't change the past, you can only work on this moment. Focus on what you can do instead of what you can't.

Babies aren't born learning to walk. They are growing and developing daily and we celebrate these accomplishments with them! We get excited and encourage them when they smile, roll over, sit up, crawl, talk, and take their first steps. When a baby falls down, we don't yell at them or turn our back on them. We encourage them, pick them back up and work with them. We know this is a process and after a short time, they will develop the muscles and coordination that will help them run, climb, and jump.

Give yourself permission to "not be perfect" and if you fall, pick yourself back up and brush yourself off and go after it again… and again… and again until you get the results you want.

Each section is set up as a weekly plan. **Beginning of the week – know what you want. It is time to be the author of your life:**

1. Set up your goals and write out why these are important to you. If they aren't important, human nature is to take the path of least resistance and all good intentions get set aside when something we deem as "more important" creeps in.

2. Create a consequence if you don't follow through with your goals. The reason behind this, we are motivated by pain and pleasure. We shy away from pain and gravitate toward pleasure (what it easy). When you create a consequence that is embarrassing and/or painful, the focus becomes on making sure the goals are completed.

    Examples of consequences: Wear a tutu to the gym, have your child paint your nails and wear the nail polish to work, stand on a busy corner and sing a song, wear P.J.'s to work, can't wear any make-up, sing a song / do a dance at a company meeting while being videotaped, let your child pick out what you're wearing for the day, etc.

3. Create an accountability partner/system. Let someone know what you're committing to do. The power of support is incredible! It gives us the extra push when things get hard. There is strength in numbers!

Daily journaling:

1. **What is important to remember.** This is a great place to write your favorite quote, scripture, mantra, intention, etc.

2. **Affirmations.** Affirmations are powerful! What we think about we bring about. It is time to be intentional and focus on who you are and what you want.

3. **Gratitude.** What are you grateful for? Studies show that people who regularly practice gratitude by taking time to notice and reflect upon the things they're thankful for, experience more positive emotions, feel more alive, sleep better, express more compassion and kindness, and even have stronger immune systems.

4. **Three (3) most important things to do today.** You already set up your weekly goals. The daily action plan helps you create the success of these goals. What are the three most important things you must do today that will help set you up for success? This gives you a blueprint and an area of focus.

5. **Thoughts/Feelings/Insights.** This is a place to freely write what's on your mind. What are you thinking, feeling, what are you aware of, what do you need to remind yourself of?

6. **I am proud of myself.** It's important to be your own cheerleader. What did you accomplish the day before or this day that you're proud of? We beat ourselves up enough about what we don't do. It's important to recognize and celebrate who we are and what we do!

There are seven daily journaling plans per week and two blank pages to write whatever you want. This is your place, your space. Make it what you want.

> What if
> I Fall?
>
> Oh, my
> Darling,
> What if
> You fly?

Affirmations

Affirmations are about our self-talk aimed at instilling positive messages and outcomes. It is the declaration that something is true   A truth you want to remember, a truth to live by, a truth to inspire or a truth to motivate.

Our lives are a byproduct of our beliefs and it is our beliefs that determine how we feel, the actions we take and how we speak to ourselves.

Affirmations are powerful! What we think about we bring about.   It is time to be intentional and focus on who you are and what you want.

Ideas for Affirmations:
I am BOLD
I am beautiful inside and out
I LOVE me!
I am creative and brilliant
I am confident in who I am
I am a team player
I am valuable and worth living the life I want
I am a powerful communicator. I listen intently, ask questions, and am clear with my thoughts
I am blessed beyond measure and am attracting the right people and opportunities into my life
I love and except myself just the way I am
I connect with people
I am amazing at building relationships
I love what I do
I am a powerful role model. My words and actions are in alignment.
I am a light
I am authentic
I am courageous and face my fears
I trust myself
I am a gift to this world
I am attracting abundance and am a wise steward of my finances
I am at peace
I forgive myself
I am compassionate and seek to understand others
I let go of the past and focus on what I can control
I am alive!
I am healthy and take loving care of my body
I am aware of my attitude and emotions

I AM...

Who are you? What gifts, strengths and talents do you have?

I AM...

Talents (What do you do effortlessly, what comes easy to you?)	
Attributes (qualities, characteristics)	
Values (what do you stand for)	
Who Do Others Say You Are? (What can they count on you for? What talents and abilities would they say you have?)	

"The one thing that you have that nobody else has is YOU.

Your voice, your mind, your story, your vision.

So, WRITE and DRAW and PLAY and DANCE and LIVE only as you can!"

~ Neil Gaiman

"Powerful Beyond Measure"

"Our deepest fear is not that we are inadequate. Our deepest fear is that we are powerful beyond measure. It is our light, not our darkness that most frightens us. We ask ourselves, who am I to be brilliant, gorgeous, talented, and fabulous? Actually, who are you not to be? You are a child of God. Your playing small does not serve the world. There is nothing enlightened about shrinking so that other people won't feel insecure around you. We are all meant to shine, as children do. We were born to make manifest the glory of God that is within us. It's not just in some of us, it's in everyone. And as we let our own light shine, we unconsciously give other people permission to do the same. As we are liberated from our own fear, our presence automatically liberates others."

~ Marianne Williamson

~ Note to self...

I'm going to make you so PROUD!

What are some things that you can do that will make YOU proud of YOU?

_____
_____
_____
_____
_____
_____
_____
_____
_____
_____
_____
_____
_____
_____

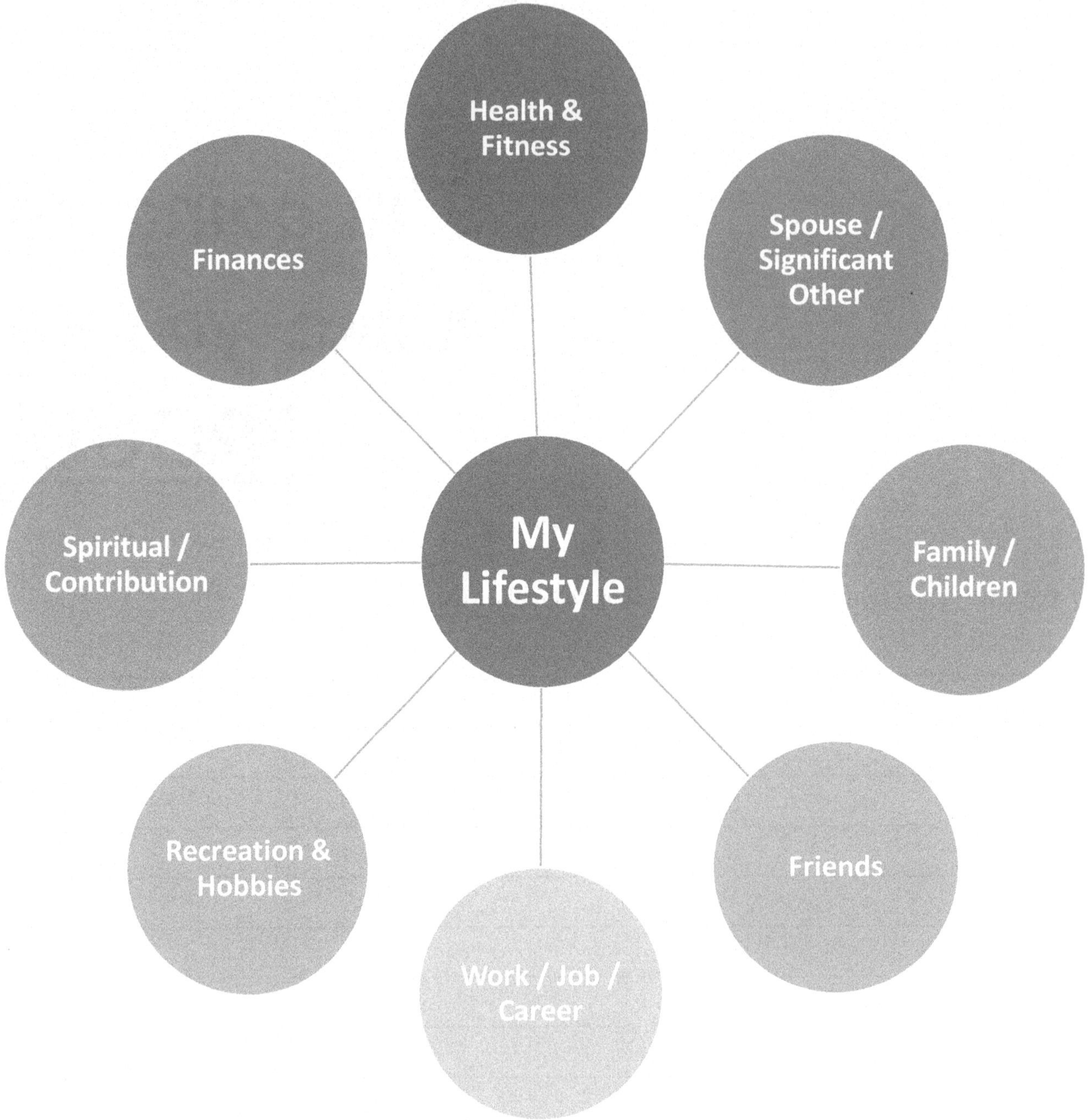
Health & Fitness
Finances
Spouse / Significant Other
My Lifestyle
Spiritual / Contribution
Family / Children
Recreation & Hobbies
Friends
Work / Job / Career

Rank yourself on a scale of 1 – 10 on how satisfied you are in these areas:

Health & Fitness   _____

Spouse / Significant Other _____

Family / Children   _____

Friends   _____

Work / Job / Career   _____

Recreation / Hobbies   _____

Spiritual / Contribution   _____

Financial   _____

What is the key piece to my balanced life which all else builds from?

A picture is worth a thousand words... use these two pages to draw in detail what you want your life to look like in the next five years. Include your relationships, career, health, finances, recreation, spiritual, etc.

My Starting Point

Today's Date _____

Where do I want to be three months from now? What matters most to me?

Health / Fitness	
Relationships	
Career	
Spiritual / Contribution	
Financial	
Recreation / Hobbies	
Other	

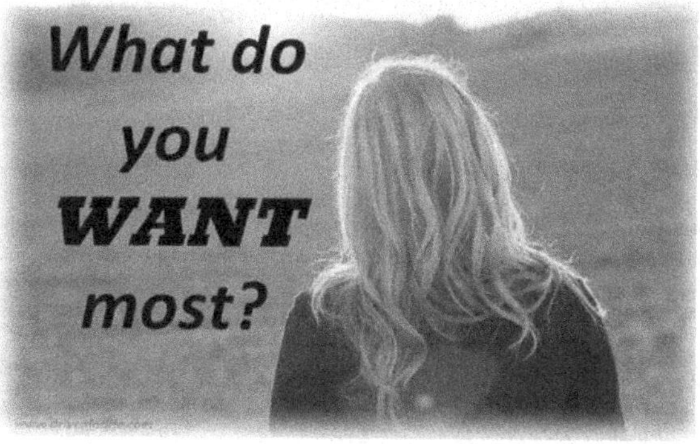
What do
you
WANT
most?

Why is this important?

live intentionally.

Date_____

My Goals for This Week That Are 100% In My Control:	**WHY** is this Important?
Personal:	
Business:	
Health:	
Other:	
Consequence if I don't hit my goals (pain and pleasure) - Be so dedicated to your goals that you will do whatever it takes to follow through. If it's important you'll make a way, if not you'll make an excuse.	

Accountability Partner: _____
(Tell someone what you're doing, create a tribe)

"Actions express priorities." ~ Mahatma Gandhi

Either YOU create the day or the day creates you…. Date _____

What is important to remember today (favorite scripture, quote, mantra, intention):

I Am_____   I Am_____

I Am_____   I Am_____

I Am_____   I Am_____

What I Am Grateful For:

What are the three (3) most important things I need to do today that will help me create the success I desire?

1.

2.

3.

Thoughts/Insights/Feelings:

I Am Proud of Myself For....

Either YOU create the day or the day creates you....   Date _____

What is important to remember today (favorite scripture, quote, mantra, intention):

I Am_____   I Am_____

I Am_____   I Am_____

I Am_____   I Am_____

What I Am Grateful For:

What are the three (3) most important things I need to do today that will help me create the success I desire?

1.

2.

3.

Thoughts/Insights/Feelings:

I Am Proud of Myself For….

Either YOU create the day or the day creates you….　　　　　　　　　　Date _____

What is important to remember today (favorite scripture, quote, mantra, intention):

I Am_____　　　I Am_____

I Am_____　　　I Am_____

I Am_____　　　I Am_____

What I Am Grateful For:

What are the three (3) most important things I need to do today that will help me create the success I desire?

1.

2.

3.

- 22 -

Thoughts/Insights/Feelings:

I Am Proud of Myself For….

Either YOU create the day or the day creates you....   Date _____

What is important to remember today (favorite scripture, quote, mantra, intention):

I Am_____   I Am_____

I Am_____   I Am_____

I Am_____   I Am_____

What I Am Grateful For:

What are the three (3) most important things I need to do today that will help me create the success I desire?

1.

2.

3.

Thoughts/Insights/Feelings:

I Am Proud of Myself For....

Either YOU create the day or the day creates you…. Date _____

What is important to remember today (favorite scripture, quote, mantra, intention):

I Am_____   I Am_____

I Am_____   I Am_____

I Am_____   I Am_____

What I Am Grateful For:

What are the three (3) most important things I need to do today that will help me create the success I desire?

1.

2.

3.

Thoughts/Insights/Feelings:

I Am Proud of Myself For….

Either YOU create the day or the day creates you….   Date _____

What is important to remember today (favorite scripture, quote, mantra, intention):

I Am_____   I Am_____

I Am_____   I Am_____

I Am_____   I Am_____

What I Am Grateful For:

What are the three (3) most important things I need to do today that will help me create the success I desire?

1.

2.

3.

Thoughts/Insights/Feelings:

I Am Proud of Myself For....

Either YOU create the day or the day creates you….   Date _____

What do I need to remind myself of today (favorite scripture, quote, mantra, intention)?

I Am_____   I Am_____

I Am_____   I Am_____

I Am_____   I Am_____

What I Am Grateful For:

What are the three (3) most important things I need to do today that will help me create the success I desire?

1.

2.

3.

Thoughts/Insights/Feelings:

I Am Proud of Myself For....

There's that moment every morning when you look in the mirror:

Are you committed, or are you not?

~ Lebron James

Date_____

My Goals for This Week That Are 100% In My Control:	**WHY** is this Important?
Personal:	
Business:	
Health:	
Other:	

Consequence if I don't hit my goals (pain and pleasure) - Be so dedicated to your goals that you will do whatever it takes to follow through. If it's important you'll make a way, if not you'll make an excuse.	

Accountability Partner: _____
(Tell someone what you're doing, create a tribe)

"Push that snooze button and you'll end up working for someone who didn't." ~ Eric Thomas

Either YOU create the day or the day creates you....   Date _____

What is important to remember today (favorite scripture, quote, mantra, intention):

I Am_____   I Am_____

I Am_____   I Am_____

I Am_____   I Am_____

What I Am Grateful For:

What are the three (3) most important things I need to do today that will help me create the success I desire?

1.

2.

3.

Thoughts/Insights/Feelings:

I Am Proud of Myself For....

Either YOU create the day or the day creates you….   Date _____

What is important to remember today (favorite scripture, quote, mantra, intention):

I Am_____   I Am_____

I Am_____   I Am_____

I Am_____   I Am_____

What I Am Grateful For:

What are the three (3) most important things I need to do today that will help me create the success I desire?

1.

2.

3.

Thoughts/Insights/Feelings:

I Am Proud of Myself For....

Either YOU create the day or the day creates you…. Date _____

What is important to remember today (favorite scripture, quote, mantra, intention):

I Am_____ I Am_____

I Am_____ I Am_____

I Am_____ I Am_____

What I Am Grateful For:

What are the three (3) most important things I need to do today that will help me create the success I desire?

1.

2.

3.

Thoughts/Insights/Feelings:

I Am Proud of Myself For….

Either YOU create the day or the day creates you….   Date _____

What is important to remember today (favorite scripture, quote, mantra, intention):

I Am_____   I Am_____

I Am_____   I Am_____

I Am_____   I Am_____

What I Am Grateful For:

What are the three (3) most important things I need to do today that will help me create the success I desire?

1.

2.

3.

Thoughts/Insights/Feelings:

I Am Proud of Myself For….

Either YOU create the day or the day creates you….   Date _____

What is important to remember today (favorite scripture, quote, mantra, intention):

I Am_____   I Am_____

I Am_____   I Am_____

I Am_____   I Am_____

What I Am Grateful For:

What are the three (3) most important things I need to do today that will help me create the success I desire?

1.

2.

3.

Thoughts/Insights/Feelings:

I Am Proud of Myself For....

Either YOU create the day or the day creates you…. Date _____

What is important to remember today (favorite scripture, quote, mantra, intention):

I Am_____   I Am_____

I Am_____   I Am_____

I Am_____   I Am_____

What I Am Grateful For:

What are the three (3) most important things I need to do today that will help me create the success I desire?

1.

2.

3.

Thoughts/Insights/Feelings:

I Am Proud of Myself For….

Either YOU create the day or the day creates you…. Date _____

What is important to remember today (favorite scripture, quote, mantra, intention):

I Am_____ I Am_____

I Am_____ I Am_____

I Am_____ I Am_____

What I Am Grateful For:

What are the three (3) most important things I need to do today that will help me create the success I desire?

1.

2.

3.

Thoughts/Insights/Feelings:

I Am Proud of Myself For….

"The project you are most resisting carries your greatest growth."

– Robin Sharma

Date_____

My Goals for This Week That Are 100% In My Control:	**WHY** is this Important?
Personal:	
Business:	
Health:	
Other:	

| **Consequence** if I don't hit my goals (pain and pleasure) - Be so dedicated to your goals that you will do whatever it takes to follow through. If it's important you'll make a way, if not you'll make an excuse. | |

Accountability Partner: _____
(Tell someone what you're doing, create a tribe)

"There is no dishonor in losing the race. There is dishonor in not racing because you are afraid to lose."
~Garth Stein

Either YOU create the day or the day creates you…. Date _____

What is important to remember today (favorite scripture, quote, mantra, intention):

I Am_____   I Am_____

I Am_____   I Am_____

I Am_____   I Am_____

What I Am Grateful For:

What are the three (3) most important things I need to do today that will help me create the success I desire?

1.

2.

3.

Thoughts/Insights/Feelings:

I Am Proud of Myself For….

Either YOU create the day or the day creates you.... Date _____

What is important to remember today (favorite scripture, quote, mantra, intention):

I Am_____   I Am_____

I Am_____   I Am_____

I Am_____   I Am_____

What I Am Grateful For:

What are the three (3) most important things I need to do today that will help me create the success I desire?

1.

2.

3.

Thoughts/Insights/Feelings:

I Am Proud of Myself For….

Either YOU create the day or the day creates you….   Date _____

What is important to remember today (favorite scripture, quote, mantra, intention):

I Am_____   I Am_____

I Am_____   I Am_____

I Am_____   I Am_____

What I Am Grateful For:

What are the three (3) most important things I need to do today that will help me create the success I desire?

1.

2.

3.

Thoughts/Insights/Feelings:

I Am Proud of Myself For….

Either YOU create the day or the day creates you….   Date _____

What is important to remember today (favorite scripture, quote, mantra, intention):

I Am_____   I Am_____

I Am_____   I Am_____

I Am_____   I Am_____

What I Am Grateful For:

What are the three (3) most important things I need to do today that will help me create the success I desire?

1.

2.

3.

Thoughts/Insights/Feelings:

I Am Proud of Myself For....

Either YOU create the day or the day creates you…. Date _____

What is important to remember today (favorite scripture, quote, mantra, intention):

I Am_____   I Am_____

I Am_____   I Am_____

I Am_____   I Am_____

What I Am Grateful For:

What are the three (3) most important things I need to do today that will help me create the success I desire?

1.

2.

3.

Thoughts/Insights/Feelings:

I Am Proud of Myself For….

Either YOU create the day or the day creates you…. Date _____

What is important to remember today (favorite scripture, quote, mantra, intention):

I Am_____   I Am_____

I Am_____   I Am_____

I Am_____   I Am_____

What I Am Grateful For:

What are the three (3) most important things I need to do today that will help me create the success I desire?

1.

2.

3.

Thoughts/Insights/Feelings:

I Am Proud of Myself For....

Either YOU create the day or the day creates you.... Date _____

What is important to remember today (favorite scripture, quote, mantra, intention):

I Am_____   I Am_____

I Am_____   I Am_____

I Am_____   I Am_____

What I Am Grateful For:

What are the three (3) most important things I need to do today that will help me create the success I desire?

1.

2.

3.

Thoughts/Insights/Feelings:

I Am Proud of Myself For....

I Am...
Brave
Fearless
BOLD &
Strong

Date_____

My Goals for This Week That Are 100% In My Control:	**WHY** is this Important?
Personal:	
Business:	
Health:	
Other:	

Consequence if I don't hit my goals (pain and pleasure) - Be so dedicated to your goals that you will do whatever it takes to follow through. If it's important you'll make a way, if not you'll make an excuse.	

Accountability Partner: _____
(Tell someone what you're doing, create a tribe)

"Men's best successes come after their disappointments." ~ Henry Ward Beecher

Either YOU create the day or the day creates you….   Date _____

What is important to remember today (favorite scripture, quote, mantra, intention):

I Am_____   I Am_____

I Am_____   I Am_____

I Am_____   I Am_____

What I Am Grateful For:

What are the three (3) most important things I need to do today that will help me create the success I desire?

1.

2.

3.

Thoughts/Insights/Feelings:

I Am Proud of Myself For….

Either YOU create the day or the day creates you….   Date _____

What is important to remember today (favorite scripture, quote, mantra, intention):

I Am_____   I Am_____

I Am_____   I Am_____

I Am_____   I Am_____

What I Am Grateful For:

What are the three (3) most important things I need to do today that will help me create the success I desire?

1.

2.

3.

Thoughts/Insights/Feelings:

I Am Proud of Myself For….

Either YOU create the day or the day creates you….   Date _____

What is important to remember today (favorite scripture, quote, mantra, intention):

I Am_____   I Am_____

I Am_____   I Am_____

I Am_____   I Am_____

What I Am Grateful For:

What are the three (3) most important things I need to do today that will help me create the success I desire?

1.

2.

3.

Thoughts/Insights/Feelings:

I Am Proud of Myself For....

Either YOU create the day or the day creates you….   Date _____

What is important to remember today (favorite scripture, quote, mantra, intention):

I Am_____   I Am_____

I Am_____   I Am_____

I Am_____   I Am_____

What I Am Grateful For:

What are the three (3) most important things I need to do today that will help me create the success I desire?

1.

2.

3.

Thoughts/Insights/Feelings:

I Am Proud of Myself For….

Either YOU create the day or the day creates you…. Date _____

What is important to remember today (favorite scripture, quote, mantra, intention):

I Am_____ I Am_____

I Am_____ I Am_____

I Am_____ I Am_____

What I Am Grateful For:

What are the three (3) most important things I need to do today that will help me create the success I desire?

1.

2.

3.

Thoughts/Insights/Feelings:

I Am Proud of Myself For….

Either YOU create the day or the day creates you….   Date _____

What is important to remember today (favorite scripture, quote, mantra, intention):

I Am_____   I Am_____

I Am_____   I Am_____

I Am_____   I Am_____

What I Am Grateful For:

What are the three (3) most important things I need to do today that will help me create the success I desire?

1.

2.

3.

Thoughts/Insights/Feelings:

I Am Proud of Myself For….

Either YOU create the day or the day creates you....   Date _____

What is important to remember today (favorite scripture, quote, mantra, intention):

I Am_____   I Am_____

I Am_____   I Am_____

I Am_____   I Am_____

What I Am Grateful For:

What are the three (3) most important things I need to do today that will help me create the success I desire?

1.

2.

3.

Thoughts/Insights/Feelings:

I Am Proud of Myself For....

One Month Check Point

Today's Date _____

How am I doing on my three-month plan?

Health / Fitness	
Relationships	
Career	
Spiritual / Contribution	
Financial	
Recreation / Hobbies	
Other	

What's working?

What are my challenges?

What do I need to:

Start Doing	**Stop Doing**	**Continue Doing**

"It's okay if you fall down and lose your spark. Just make sure that when you get back up, you rise as the whole damn fire."

— Colette Werden

Date_____

My Goals for This Week That Are 100% In My Control:	**WHY** is this Important?
Personal:	
Business:	
Health:	
Other:	
Consequence if I don't hit my goals (pain and pleasure) - Be so dedicated to your goals that you will do whatever it takes to follow through. If it's important you'll make a way, if not you'll make an excuse.	

Accountability Partner: _____
(Tell someone what you're doing, create a tribe)

"Strength shows, not only in the ability to persist, but the ability to start over." ~ Unknown

Either YOU create the day or the day creates you.... Date _____

What is important to remember today (favorite scripture, quote, mantra, intention):

I Am_____   I Am_____

I Am_____   I Am_____

I Am_____   I Am_____

What I Am Grateful For:

What are the three (3) most important things I need to do today that will help me create the success I desire?

1.

2.

3.

Thoughts/Insights/Feelings:

I Am Proud of Myself For….

Either YOU create the day or the day creates you…. Date _____

What is important to remember today (favorite scripture, quote, mantra, intention):

I Am_____   I Am_____

I Am_____   I Am_____

I Am_____   I Am_____

What I Am Grateful For:

What are the three (3) most important things I need to do today that will help me create the success I desire?

1.

2.

3.

Thoughts/Insights/Feelings:

I Am Proud of Myself For….

Either YOU create the day or the day creates you…. Date _____

What is important to remember today (favorite scripture, quote, mantra, intention):

I Am_____   I Am_____

I Am_____   I Am_____

I Am_____   I Am_____

What I Am Grateful For:

What are the three (3) most important things I need to do today that will help me create the success I desire?

1.

2.

3.

Thoughts/Insights/Feelings:

I Am Proud of Myself For....

Either YOU create the day or the day creates you….   Date _____

What is important to remember today (favorite scripture, quote, mantra, intention):

I Am_____   I Am_____

I Am_____   I Am_____

I Am_____   I Am_____

What I Am Grateful For:

What are the three (3) most important things I need to do today that will help me create the success I desire?

1.

2.

3.

Thoughts/Insights/Feelings:

I Am Proud of Myself For....

Either YOU create the day or the day creates you….   Date _____

What is important to remember today (favorite scripture, quote, mantra, intention):

I Am_____   I Am_____

I Am_____   I Am_____

I Am_____   I Am_____

What I Am Grateful For:

What are the three (3) most important things I need to do today that will help me create the success I desire?

1.

2.

3.

Thoughts/Insights/Feelings:

I Am Proud of Myself For….

Either YOU create the day or the day creates you….   Date _____

What is important to remember today (favorite scripture, quote, mantra, intention):

I Am_____   I Am_____

I Am_____   I Am_____

I Am_____   I Am_____

What I Am Grateful For:

What are the three (3) most important things I need to do today that will help me create the success I desire?

1.

2.

3.

Thoughts/Insights/Feelings:

I Am Proud of Myself For….

Either YOU create the day or the day creates you.... Date _____

What is important to remember today (favorite scripture, quote, mantra, intention):

I Am_____   I Am_____

I Am_____   I Am_____

I Am_____   I Am_____

What I Am Grateful For:

What are the three (3) most important things I need to do today that will help me create the success I desire?

1.

2.

3.

Thoughts/Insights/Feelings:

I Am Proud of Myself For….

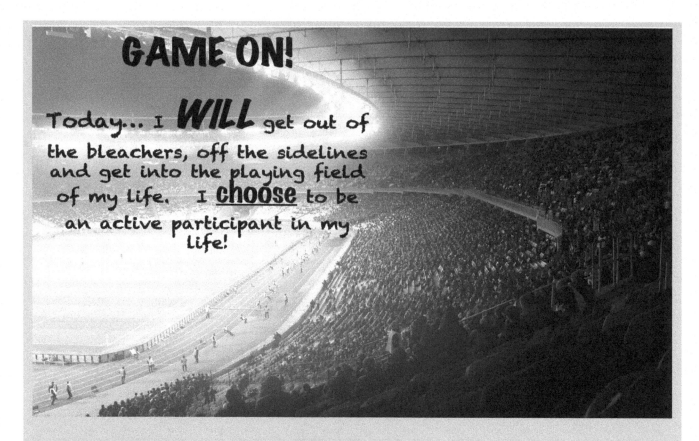

Today I Will:

Why this is important to me:

Date_____

My Goals for This Week That Are 100% In My Control:	**WHY** is this Important?
Personal:	
Business:	
Health:	
Other:	

| **Consequence** if I don't hit my goals (pain and pleasure) - Be so dedicated to your goals that you will do whatever it takes to follow through. If it's important you'll make a way, if not you'll make an excuse. | |

Accountability Partner: _____
(Tell someone what you're doing, create a tribe)

"If it is important to you, you will find a way. If not you'll find an excuse." ~ Unknown

Either YOU create the day or the day creates you….   Date _____

What is important to remember today (favorite scripture, quote, mantra, intention):

I Am_____   I Am_____

I Am_____   I Am_____

I Am_____   I Am_____

What I Am Grateful For:

What are the three (3) most important things I need to do today that will help me create the success I desire?

1.

2.

3.

Thoughts/Insights/Feelings:

I Am Proud of Myself For....

Either YOU create the day or the day creates you…. Date _____

What is important to remember today (favorite scripture, quote, mantra, intention):

I Am_____   I Am_____

I Am_____   I Am_____

I Am_____   I Am_____

What I Am Grateful For:

What are the three (3) most important things I need to do today that will help me create the success I desire?

1.

2.

3.

- 112 -

Thoughts/Insights/Feelings:

I Am Proud of Myself For....

Either YOU create the day or the day creates you.... Date _____

What is important to remember today (favorite scripture, quote, mantra, intention):

I Am_____   I Am_____

I Am_____   I Am_____

I Am_____   I Am_____

What I Am Grateful For:

What are the three (3) most important things I need to do today that will help me create the success I desire?

1.

2.

3.

Thoughts/Insights/Feelings:

I Am Proud of Myself For….

Either YOU create the day or the day creates you….　　　　　　　　　Date _____

What is important to remember today (favorite scripture, quote, mantra, intention):

I Am_____　　　I Am_____

I Am_____　　　I Am_____

I Am_____　　　I Am_____

What I Am Grateful For:

What are the three (3) most important things I need to do today that will help me create the success I desire?

1.

2.

3.

Thoughts/Insights/Feelings:

I Am Proud of Myself For….

Either YOU create the day or the day creates you…. Date _____

What is important to remember today (favorite scripture, quote, mantra, intention):

I Am_____   I Am_____

I Am_____   I Am_____

I Am_____   I Am_____

What I Am Grateful For:

What are the three (3) most important things I need to do today that will help me create the success I desire?

1.

2.

3.

Thoughts/Insights/Feelings:

I Am Proud of Myself For….

Either YOU create the day or the day creates you.... Date _____

What is important to remember today (favorite scripture, quote, mantra, intention):

I Am_____   I Am_____

I Am_____   I Am_____

I Am_____   I Am_____

What I Am Grateful For:

What are the three (3) most important things I need to do today that will help me create the success I desire?

1.

2.

3.

Thoughts/Insights/Feelings:

I Am Proud of Myself For….

Either YOU create the day or the day creates you….   Date _____

What is important to remember today (favorite scripture, quote, mantra, intention):

I Am_____   I Am_____

I Am_____   I Am_____

I Am_____   I Am_____

What I Am Grateful For:

What are the three (3) most important things I need to do today that will help me create the success I desire?

1.

2.

3.

Thoughts/Insights/Feelings:

I Am Proud of Myself For….

Today I will...

I am...

Date_____

My Goals for This Week That Are 100% In My Control:	**WHY** is this Important?
Personal:	
Business:	
Health:	
Other:	

Consequence if I don't hit my goals (pain and pleasure) - Be so dedicated to your goals that you will do whatever it takes to follow through. If it's important you'll make a way, if not you'll make an excuse.	

Accountability Partner: _____
(Tell someone what you're doing, create a tribe)

"If you hear a voice within you say, "You cannot paint," then by all means paint, and that voice will be silenced."
~ Vincent van Gogh

Either YOU create the day or the day creates you….   Date _____

What is important to remember today (favorite scripture, quote, mantra, intention):

I Am_____   I Am_____

I Am_____   I Am_____

I Am_____   I Am_____

What I Am Grateful For:

What are the three (3) most important things I need to do today that will help me create the success I desire?

1.

2.

3.

Thoughts/Insights/Feelings:

I Am Proud of Myself For....

Either YOU create the day or the day creates you….   Date _____

What is important to remember today (favorite scripture, quote, mantra, intention):

I Am_____   I Am_____

I Am_____   I Am_____

I Am_____   I Am_____

What I Am Grateful For:

What are the three (3) most important things I need to do today that will help me create the success I desire?

1.

2.

3.

Thoughts/Insights/Feelings:

I Am Proud of Myself For....

Either YOU create the day or the day creates you….   Date _____

What is important to remember today (favorite scripture, quote, mantra, intention):

I Am_____   I Am_____

I Am_____   I Am_____

I Am_____   I Am_____

What I Am Grateful For:

What are the three (3) most important things I need to do today that will help me create the success I desire?

1.

2.

3.

Thoughts/Insights/Feelings:

I Am Proud of Myself For….

Either YOU create the day or the day creates you…. Date _____

What is important to remember today (favorite scripture, quote, mantra, intention):

I Am_____   I Am_____

I Am_____   I Am_____

I Am_____   I Am_____

What I Am Grateful For:

What are the three (3) most important things I need to do today that will help me create the success I desire?

1.

2.

3.

Thoughts/Insights/Feelings:

I Am Proud of Myself For….

Either YOU create the day or the day creates you…. Date _____

What is important to remember today (favorite scripture, quote, mantra, intention):

I Am_____   I Am_____

I Am_____   I Am_____

I Am_____   I Am_____

What I Am Grateful For:

What are the three (3) most important things I need to do today that will help me create the success I desire?

1.

2.

3.

Thoughts/Insights/Feelings:

I Am Proud of Myself For….

Either YOU create the day or the day creates you.... Date _____

What is important to remember today (favorite scripture, quote, mantra, intention):

I Am_____   I Am_____

I Am_____   I Am_____

I Am_____   I Am_____

What I Am Grateful For:

What are the three (3) most important things I need to do today that will help me create the success I desire?

1.

2.

3.

Thoughts/Insights/Feelings:

I Am Proud of Myself For....

Either YOU create the day or the day creates you.... Date _____

What is important to remember today (favorite scripture, quote, mantra, intention):

I Am_____   I Am_____

I Am_____   I Am_____

I Am_____   I Am_____

What I Am Grateful For:

What are the three (3) most important things I need to do today that will help me create the success I desire?

1.

2.

3.

Thoughts/Insights/Feelings:

I Am Proud of Myself For….

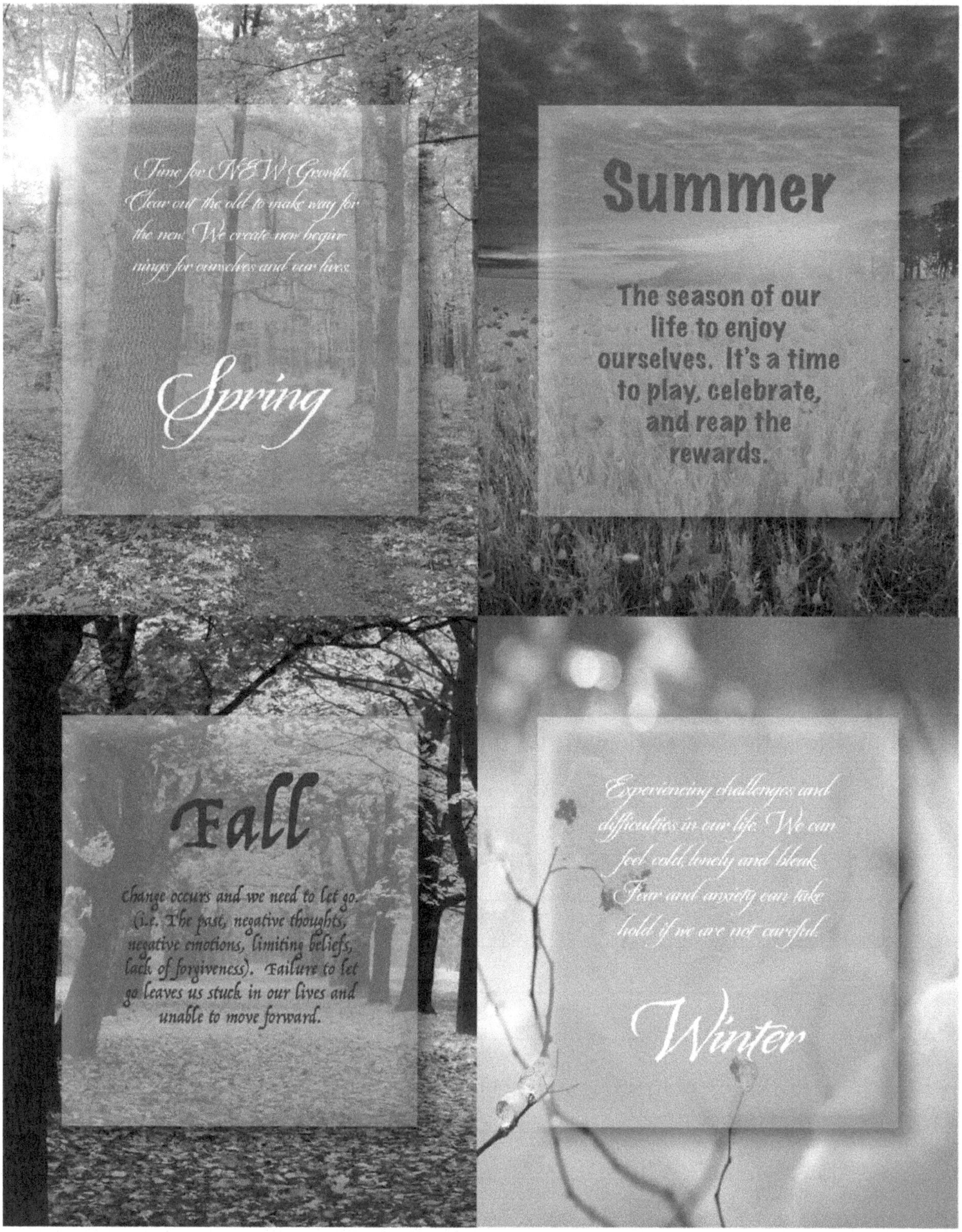
Time for NEW Growth.
Clear out the old to make way for the new. We create new beginnings for ourselves and our lives.
Spring
Summer
The season of our life to enjoy ourselves. It's a time to play, celebrate, and reap the rewards.
Fall
Change occurs and we need to let go. (i.e. The past, negative thoughts, negative emotions, limiting beliefs, lack of forgiveness). Failure to let go leaves us stuck in our lives and unable to move forward.
Experiencing challenges and difficulties in our life. We can feel cold, lonely and bleak. Fear and anxiety can take hold if we are not careful.
Winter

Seasons in Life

List your experiences in the last five (5) years in these different seasons:

Spring (new growth)	
Summer (celebrate / play)	
Fall (change / let go)	
Winter (challenges / difficulties)	

What season am I in now?

What do I need to remind myself of where I'm at right now within this season?

Date _____

My Goals for This Week That Are 100% In My Control:	**WHY** is this Important?
Personal:	
Business:	
Health:	
Other:	

| **Consequence** if I don't hit my goals (pain and pleasure) -   Be so dedicated to your goals that you will do whatever it takes to follow through. If it's important you'll make a way, if not you'll make an excuse. | |

Accountability Partner: _____
(Tell someone what you're doing, create a tribe)

"No sun outlasts its sunset but will rise again and bring the dawn." ~ Maya Angelou

Either YOU create the day or the day creates you…. Date _____

What is important to remember today (favorite scripture, quote, mantra, intention):

I Am_____   I Am_____

I Am_____   I Am_____

I Am_____   I Am_____

What I Am Grateful For:

What are the three (3) most important things I need to do today that will help me create the success I desire?

1.

2.

3.

Thoughts/Insights/Feelings:

I Am Proud of Myself For….

Either YOU create the day or the day creates you….   Date _____

What is important to remember today (favorite scripture, quote, mantra, intention):

I Am_____   I Am_____

I Am_____   I Am_____

I Am_____   I Am_____

What I Am Grateful For:

What are the three (3) most important things I need to do today that will help me create the success I desire?

1.

2.

3.

Thoughts/Insights/Feelings:

I Am Proud of Myself For....

Either YOU create the day or the day creates you….   Date _____

What is important to remember today (favorite scripture, quote, mantra, intention):

I Am_____   I Am_____

I Am_____   I Am_____

I Am_____   I Am_____

What I Am Grateful For:

What are the three (3) most important things I need to do today that will help me create the success I desire?

1.

2.

3.

Thoughts/Insights/Feelings:

I Am Proud of Myself For....

Either YOU create the day or the day creates you.... Date _____

What is important to remember today (favorite scripture, quote, mantra, intention):

I Am_____   I Am_____

I Am_____   I Am_____

I Am_____   I Am_____

What I Am Grateful For:

What are the three (3) most important things I need to do today that will help me create the success I desire?

1.

2.

3.

Thoughts/Insights/Feelings:

I Am Proud of Myself For....

Either YOU create the day or the day creates you….   Date _____

What is important to remember today (favorite scripture, quote, mantra, intention):

I Am_____   I Am_____

I Am_____   I Am_____

I Am_____   I Am_____

What I Am Grateful For:

What are the three (3) most important things I need to do today that will help me create the success I desire?

1.

2.

3.

Thoughts/Insights/Feelings:

I Am Proud of Myself For….

Either YOU create the day or the day creates you.... Date _____

What is important to remember today (favorite scripture, quote, mantra, intention):

I Am_____   I Am_____

I Am_____   I Am_____

I Am_____   I Am_____

What I Am Grateful For:

What are the three (3) most important things I need to do today that will help me create the success I desire?

1.

2.

3.

Thoughts/Insights/Feelings:

I Am Proud of Myself For....

Either YOU create the day or the day creates you….   Date _____

What is important to remember today (favorite scripture, quote, mantra, intention):

I Am_____   I Am_____

I Am_____   I Am_____

I Am_____   I Am_____

What I Am Grateful For:

What are the three (3) most important things I need to do today that will help me create the success I desire?

1.

2.

3.

Thoughts/Insights/Feelings:

I Am Proud of Myself For….

If you could live one day of your life over again,

Which day would you choose?

Two Month Check Point

Today's Date _____

How am I doing on my three-month plan?

Health / Fitness	
Relationships	
Career	
Spiritual / Contribution	
Financial	
Recreation / Hobbies	
Other	

What's Working?   **What Are My Challenges?**

What do I need to:

| Start Doing | Stop Doing | Continue Doing |

Nothing Changes
IF
Nothing Changes

What's an area in my life that I am unhappy with and want different results?

What needs to change?

What actions are necessary to take to create change?

Date_____

My Goals for This Week That Are 100% In My Control:	WHY is this Important?
Personal:	
Business:	
Health:	
Other:	

Consequence if I don't hit my goals (pain and pleasure) - Be so dedicated to your goals that you will do whatever it takes to follow through. If it's important you'll make a way, if not you'll make an excuse.	

Accountability Partner: _____
(Tell someone what you're doing, create a tribe)

"When a flower doesn't bloom, you fix the environment in which it grows, not the flower." ~ Unknown

Either YOU create the day or the day creates you….   Date _____

What is important to remember today (favorite scripture, quote, mantra, intention):

I Am_____   I Am_____

I Am_____   I Am_____

I Am_____   I Am_____

What I Am Grateful For:

What are the three (3) most important things I need to do today that will help me create the success I desire?

1.

2.

3.

Thoughts/Insights/Feelings:

I Am Proud of Myself For….

Either YOU create the day or the day creates you…. Date _____

What is important to remember today (favorite scripture, quote, mantra, intention):

I Am_____   I Am_____

I Am_____   I Am_____

I Am_____   I Am_____

What I Am Grateful For:

What are the three (3) most important things I need to do today that will help me create the success I desire?

1.

2.

3.

Thoughts/Insights/Feelings:

I Am Proud of Myself For….

Either YOU create the day or the day creates you….   Date _____

What is important to remember today (favorite scripture, quote, mantra, intention):

I Am_____   I Am_____

I Am_____   I Am_____

I Am_____   I Am_____

What I Am Grateful For:

What are the three (3) most important things I need to do today that will help me create the success I desire?

1.

2.

3.

Thoughts/Insights/Feelings:

I Am Proud of Myself For....

Either YOU create the day or the day creates you….   Date _____

What is important to remember today (favorite scripture, quote, mantra, intention):

I Am_____   I Am_____

I Am_____   I Am_____

I Am_____   I Am_____

What I Am Grateful For:

What are the three (3) most important things I need to do today that will help me create the success I desire?

1.

2.

3.

Thoughts/Insights/Feelings:

I Am Proud of Myself For….

Either YOU create the day or the day creates you.... Date _____

What is important to remember today (favorite scripture, quote, mantra, intention):

I Am_____   I Am_____

I Am_____   I Am_____

I Am_____   I Am_____

What I Am Grateful For:

What are the three (3) most important things I need to do today that will help me create the success I desire?

1.

2.

3.

Thoughts/Insights/Feelings:

I Am Proud of Myself For....

Either YOU create the day or the day creates you....   Date _____

What is important to remember today (favorite scripture, quote, mantra, intention):

I Am_____   I Am_____

I Am_____   I Am_____

I Am_____   I Am_____

What I Am Grateful For:

What are the three (3) most important things I need to do today that will help me create the success I desire?

1.

2.

3.

Thoughts/Insights/Feelings:

I Am Proud of Myself For....

Either YOU create the day or the day creates you…. Date _____

What is important to remember today (favorite scripture, quote, mantra, intention):

I Am_____   I Am_____

I Am_____   I Am_____

I Am_____   I Am_____

What I Am Grateful For:

What are the three (3) most important things I need to do today that will help me create the success I desire?

1.

2.

3.

Thoughts/Insights/Feelings:

I Am Proud of Myself For….

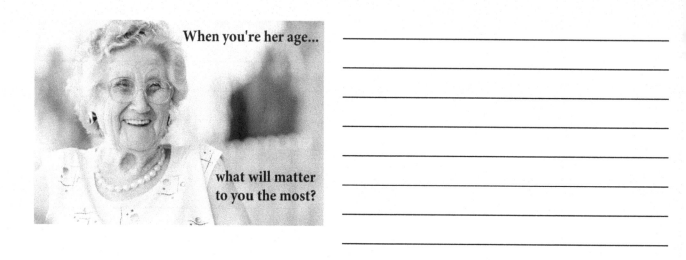

LEGACY: What kind of life do you want to live? What do you want to be remembered for? What gifts, lessons and wisdom will others gain because you have lived?

Date _____

My Goals for This Week That Are 100% In My Control:	**WHY** is this Important?
Personal:	
Business:	
Health:	
Other:	

Consequence if I don't hit my goals (pain and pleasure) - Be so dedicated to your goals that you will do whatever it takes to follow through. If it's important you'll make a way, if not you'll make an excuse.	

Accountability Partner: _____
(Tell someone what you're doing, create a tribe)

"To know even one life has breathed easier because you have lived, this is to have succeeded."
~ Ralph Waldo Emerson

Either YOU create the day or the day creates you….   Date _____

What is important to remember today (favorite scripture, quote, mantra, intention):

I Am_____   I Am_____

I Am_____   I Am_____

I Am_____   I Am_____

What I Am Grateful For:

What are the three (3) most important things I need to do today that will help me create the success I desire?

1.

2.

3.

Thoughts/Insights/Feelings:

I Am Proud of Myself For....

Either YOU create the day or the day creates you….　　　　　　　　Date _____

What is important to remember today (favorite scripture, quote, mantra, intention):

I Am_____　　　I Am_____

I Am_____　　　I Am_____

I Am_____　　　I Am_____

What I Am Grateful For:

What are the three (3) most important things I need to do today that will help me create the success I desire?

1.

2.

3.

Thoughts/Insights/Feelings:

I Am Proud of Myself For….

Either YOU create the day or the day creates you…. Date _____

What is important to remember today (favorite scripture, quote, mantra, intention):

I Am_____   I Am_____

I Am_____   I Am_____

I Am_____   I Am_____

What I Am Grateful For:

What are the three (3) most important things I need to do today that will help me create the success I desire?

1.

2.

3.

Thoughts/Insights/Feelings:

I Am Proud of Myself For….

Either YOU create the day or the day creates you….   Date _____

What is important to remember today (favorite scripture, quote, mantra, intention):

I Am_____   I Am_____

I Am_____   I Am_____

I Am_____   I Am_____

What I Am Grateful For:

What are the three (3) most important things I need to do today that will help me create the success I desire?

1.

2.

3.

Thoughts/Insights/Feelings:

I Am Proud of Myself For….

Either YOU create the day or the day creates you….   Date _____

What is important to remember today (favorite scripture, quote, mantra, intention):

I Am_____   I Am_____

I Am_____   I Am_____

I Am_____   I Am_____

What I Am Grateful For:

What are the three (3) most important things I need to do today that will help me create the success I desire?

1.

2.

3.

Thoughts/Insights/Feelings:

I Am Proud of Myself For….

Either YOU create the day or the day creates you.... Date _____

What is important to remember today (favorite scripture, quote, mantra, intention):

I Am_____   I Am_____

I Am_____   I Am_____

I Am_____   I Am_____

What I Am Grateful For:

What are the three (3) most important things I need to do today that will help me create the success I desire?

1.

2.

3.

Thoughts/Insights/Feelings:

I Am Proud of Myself For....

Either YOU create the day or the day creates you…. Date _____

What is important to remember today (favorite scripture, quote, mantra, intention):

I Am_____   I Am_____

I Am_____   I Am_____

I Am_____   I Am_____

What I Am Grateful For:

What are the three (3) most important things I need to do today that will help me create the success I desire?

1.

2.

3.

Thoughts/Insights/Feelings:

I Am Proud of Myself For….

Studies show that people who regularly practice gratitude by taking time to notice and reflect upon the things they're thankful for, experience more positive emotions, feel more alive, sleep better, express more compassion and kindness, and even have stronger immune systems.

Write in detail of a moment, person or lesson whom you're incredibly grateful for that because of this it has helped shape and change your life.

Date _____

My Goals for This Week That Are 100% In My Control:	WHY is this Important?
Personal:	
Business:	
Health:	
Other:	
Consequence if I don't hit my goals (pain and pleasure) - Be so dedicated to your goals that you will do whatever it takes to follow through. If it's important you'll make a way, if not you'll make an excuse.	

Accountability Partner: _____
(Tell someone what you're doing, create a tribe)

"Gratitude unlocks the fullness of life." ~ Melody Beattie

Either YOU create the day or the day creates you…. Date _____

What is important to remember today (favorite scripture, quote, mantra, intention):

I Am_____ I Am_____

I Am_____ I Am_____

I Am_____ I Am_____

What I Am Grateful For:

What are the three (3) most important things I need to do today that will help me create the success I desire?

1.

2.

3.

Thoughts/Insights/Feelings:

I Am Proud of Myself For....

Either YOU create the day or the day creates you....   Date _____

What is important to remember today (favorite scripture, quote, mantra, intention):

I Am_____   I Am_____

I Am_____   I Am_____

I Am_____   I Am_____

What I Am Grateful For:

What are the three (3) most important things I need to do today that will help me create the success I desire?

1.

2.

3.

Thoughts/Insights/Feelings:

I Am Proud of Myself For....

Either YOU create the day or the day creates you…. Date _____

What is important to remember today (favorite scripture, quote, mantra, intention):

I Am_____ I Am_____

I Am_____ I Am_____

I Am_____ I Am_____

What I Am Grateful For:

What are the three (3) most important things I need to do today that will help me create the success I desire?

1.

2.

3.

Thoughts/Insights/Feelings:

I Am Proud of Myself For….

Either YOU create the day or the day creates you….   Date _____

What is important to remember today (favorite scripture, quote, mantra, intention):

I Am_____   I Am_____

I Am_____   I Am_____

I Am_____   I Am_____

What I Am Grateful For:

What are the three (3) most important things I need to do today that will help me create the success I desire?

1.

2.

3.

Thoughts/Insights/Feelings:

I Am Proud of Myself For....

Either YOU create the day or the day creates you….   Date _____

What is important to remember today (favorite scripture, quote, mantra, intention):

I Am_____   I Am_____

I Am_____   I Am_____

I Am_____   I Am_____

What I Am Grateful For:

What are the three (3) most important things I need to do today that will help me create the success I desire?

1.

2.

3.

Thoughts/Insights/Feelings:

I Am Proud of Myself For….

Either YOU create the day or the day creates you....   Date _____

What is important to remember today (favorite scripture, quote, mantra, intention):

I Am_____   I Am_____

I Am_____   I Am_____

I Am_____   I Am_____

What I Am Grateful For:

What are the three (3) most important things I need to do today that will help me create the success I desire?

1.

2.

3.

Thoughts/Insights/Feelings:

I Am Proud of Myself For….

Either YOU create the day or the day creates you.... Date _____

What is important to remember today (favorite scripture, quote, mantra, intention):

I Am_____   I Am_____

I Am_____   I Am_____

I Am_____   I Am_____

What I Am Grateful For:

What are the three (3) most important things I need to do today that will help me create the success I desire?

1.

2.

3.

Thoughts/Insights/Feelings:

I Am Proud of Myself For….

The greatest act of courage is to be and own all of WHO you are.

Without apology
Without excuse
Without any masks
to cover the truth of who you really are.

OWN WHO YOU ARE!

Date _____

My Goals for This Week That Are 100% In My Control:	WHY is this Important?
Personal:	
Business:	
Health:	
Other:	
Consequence if I don't hit my goals (pain and pleasure) - Be so dedicated to your goals that you will do whatever it takes to follow through. If it's important you'll make a way, if not you'll make an excuse.	

Accountability Partner: _____
(Tell someone what you're doing, create a tribe)

"When you know yourself, you are empowered. When you accept yourself, you are invincible." ~ Tina Lifford

Either YOU create the day or the day creates you….   Date _____

What is important to remember today (favorite scripture, quote, mantra, intention):

I Am_____   I Am_____

I Am_____   I Am_____

I Am_____   I Am_____

What I Am Grateful For:

What are the three (3) most important things I need to do today that will help me create the success I desire?

1.

2.

3.

Thoughts/Insights/Feelings:

I Am Proud of Myself For….

Either YOU create the day or the day creates you....   Date _____

What is important to remember today (favorite scripture, quote, mantra, intention):

I Am_____   I Am_____

I Am_____   I Am_____

I Am_____   I Am_____

What I Am Grateful For:

What are the three (3) most important things I need to do today that will help me create the success I desire?

1.

2.

3.

Thoughts/Insights/Feelings:

I Am Proud of Myself For….

Either YOU create the day or the day creates you…. Date _____

What is important to remember today (favorite scripture, quote, mantra, intention):

I Am_____   I Am_____

I Am_____   I Am_____

I Am_____   I Am_____

What I Am Grateful For:

What are the three (3) most important things I need to do today that will help me create the success I desire?

1.

2.

3.

Thoughts/Insights/Feelings:

I Am Proud of Myself For....

Either YOU create the day or the day creates you.... Date _____

What is important to remember today (favorite scripture, quote, mantra, intention):

I Am_____   I Am_____

I Am_____   I Am_____

I Am_____   I Am_____

What I Am Grateful For:

What are the three (3) most important things I need to do today that will help me create the success I desire?

1.

2.

3.

Thoughts/Insights/Feelings:

I Am Proud of Myself For....

Either YOU create the day or the day creates you…. Date _____

What is important to remember today (favorite scripture, quote, mantra, intention):

I Am_____   I Am_____

I Am_____   I Am_____

I Am_____   I Am_____

What I Am Grateful For:

What are the three (3) most important things I need to do today that will help me create the success I desire?

1.

2.

3.

Thoughts/Insights/Feelings:

I Am Proud of Myself For….

Either YOU create the day or the day creates you....   Date _____

What is important to remember today (favorite scripture, quote, mantra, intention):

I Am_____   I Am_____

I Am_____   I Am_____

I Am_____   I Am_____

What I Am Grateful For:

What are the three (3) most important things I need to do today that will help me create the success I desire?

1.

2.

3.

Thoughts/Insights/Feelings:

I Am Proud of Myself For....

Either YOU create the day or the day creates you....   Date _____

What is important to remember today (favorite scripture, quote, mantra, intention):

I Am_____   I Am_____

I Am_____   I Am_____

I Am_____   I Am_____

What I Am Grateful For:

What are the three (3) most important things I need to do today that will help me create the success I desire?

1.

2.

3.

Thoughts/Insights/Feelings:

I Am Proud of Myself For....

Three Month Check Point

Today's Date _____

How am I doing on my three-month plan?

Health / Fitness	
Relationships	
Career	
Spiritual / Contribution	
Financial	
Recreation / Hobbies	
Other	

What's Working?   **What Are My Challenges?**

What do I need to:

Start Doing	**Stop Doing**	**Continue Doing**

Where Am I Most Up and Down?

Why?

What Do I Need to do to Create Stability?

Date _____

My Goals for This Week That Are 100% In My Control:	**WHY** is this Important?
Personal:	
Business:	
Health:	
Other:	

Consequence if I don't hit my goals (pain and pleasure) - Be so dedicated to your goals that you will do whatever it takes to follow through. If it's important you'll make a way, if not you'll make an excuse.	

Accountability Partner: _____
(Tell someone what you're doing, create a tribe)

"Discipline is just choosing between what you want now and what you want most." ~ Augusta F. Kantra

Either YOU create the day or the day creates you…. Date _____

What is important to remember today (favorite scripture, quote, mantra, intention):

I Am_____   I Am_____

I Am_____   I Am_____

I Am_____   I Am_____

What I Am Grateful For:

What are the three (3) most important things I need to do today that will help me create the success I desire?

1.

2.

3.

Thoughts/Insights/Feelings:

I Am Proud of Myself For….

Either YOU create the day or the day creates you....   Date _____

What is important to remember today (favorite scripture, quote, mantra, intention):

I Am_____   I Am_____

I Am_____   I Am_____

I Am_____   I Am_____

What I Am Grateful For:

What are the three (3) most important things I need to do today that will help me create the success I desire?

1.

2.

3.

Thoughts/Insights/Feelings:

I Am Proud of Myself For….

Either YOU create the day or the day creates you….   Date _____

What is important to remember today (favorite scripture, quote, mantra, intention):

I Am_____   I Am_____

I Am_____   I Am_____

I Am_____   I Am_____

What I Am Grateful For:

What are the three (3) most important things I need to do today that will help me create the success I desire?

1.

2.

3.

Thoughts/Insights/Feelings:

I Am Proud of Myself For….

Either YOU create the day or the day creates you….   Date _____

What is important to remember today (favorite scripture, quote, mantra, intention):

I Am_____   I Am_____

I Am_____   I Am_____

I Am_____   I Am_____

What I Am Grateful For:

What are the three (3) most important things I need to do today that will help me create the success I desire?

1.

2.

3.

Thoughts/Insights/Feelings:

I Am Proud of Myself For....

Either YOU create the day or the day creates you....   Date _____

What is important to remember today (favorite scripture, quote, mantra, intention):

I Am_____   I Am_____

I Am_____   I Am_____

I Am_____   I Am_____

What I Am Grateful For:

What are the three (3) most important things I need to do today that will help me create the success I desire?

1.

2.

3.

Thoughts/Insights/Feelings:

I Am Proud of Myself For....

Either YOU create the day or the day creates you….   Date _____

What is important to remember today (favorite scripture, quote, mantra, intention):

I Am_____   I Am_____

I Am_____   I Am_____

I Am_____   I Am_____

What I Am Grateful For:

What are the three (3) most important things I need to do today that will help me create the success I desire?

1.

2.

3.

Thoughts/Insights/Feelings:

I Am Proud of Myself For….

Either YOU create the day or the day creates you….   Date _____

What is important to remember today (favorite scripture, quote, mantra, intention):

I Am_____   I Am_____

I Am_____   I Am_____

I Am_____   I Am_____

What I Am Grateful For:

What are the three (3) most important things I need to do today that will help me create the success I desire?

1.

2.

3.

Thoughts/Insights/Feelings:

I Am Proud of Myself For....

The Power of Struggle

A man found a cocoon of a butterfly. One day a small opening appeared. He sat and watched the butterfly for several hours as it struggled to force its body through that little hole. Then it seemed to stop making any progress. It appeared as if it had gotten as far as it had and it could go no further.

Then the man decided to help the butterfly, so he took a pair of scissors and snipped off the remaining bit of the cocoon. The butterfly then emerged easily. But it had a swollen body and small, shriveled wings. The man continued to watch the butterfly because he expected that, at any moment, the wings would enlarge and expand to be able to support the body, which would contract in time.

Neither happened! In fact, the butterfly spent the rest of its life crawling around with a swollen body and shriveled wings. It never was able to fly.

What the man in his kindness and haste did not understand was that the restricting cocoon and the struggle required for the butterfly to get through the tiny opening were God's way of forcing fluid from the body of the butterfly into its wings so that it would be ready for flight once it achieved its freedom from the cocoon.

Sometimes struggles are exactly what we need in our life. If God allowed us to go through our life without any obstacles, it would cripple us. We would not be as strong as what we could have been. And we could never fly.

- Author Unknown

Date _____

My Goals for This Week That Are 100% In My Control:	**WHY** is this Important?
Personal:	
Business:	
Health:	
Other:	

| **Consequence** if I don't hit my goals (pain and pleasure) - Be so dedicated to your goals that you will do whatever it takes to follow through. If it's important you'll make a way, if not you'll make an excuse. | |

Accountability Partner: _____
(Tell someone what you're doing, create a tribe)

"I am thankful for my struggle because without it I wouldn't have stumbled across my strength." Alexandra Elle

Either YOU create the day or the day creates you....   Date _____

What is important to remember today (favorite scripture, quote, mantra, intention):

I Am_____   I Am_____

I Am_____   I Am_____

I Am_____   I Am_____

What I Am Grateful For:

What are the three (3) most important things I need to do today that will help me create the success I desire?

1.

2.

3.

Thoughts/Insights/Feelings:

I Am Proud of Myself For….

Either YOU create the day or the day creates you....   Date _____

What is important to remember today (favorite scripture, quote, mantra, intention):

I Am_____   I Am_____

I Am_____   I Am_____

I Am_____   I Am_____

What I Am Grateful For:

What are the three (3) most important things I need to do today that will help me create the success I desire?

1.

2.

3.

Thoughts/Insights/Feelings:

I Am Proud of Myself For….

Either YOU create the day or the day creates you....   Date _____

What is important to remember today (favorite scripture, quote, mantra, intention):

I Am_____   I Am_____

I Am_____   I Am_____

I Am_____   I Am_____

What I Am Grateful For:

What are the three (3) most important things I need to do today that will help me create the success I desire?

1.

2.

3.

Thoughts/Insights/Feelings:

I Am Proud of Myself For….

Either YOU create the day or the day creates you…. Date _____

What is important to remember today (favorite scripture, quote, mantra, intention):

I Am_____   I Am_____

I Am_____   I Am_____

I Am_____   I Am_____

What I Am Grateful For:

What are the three (3) most important things I need to do today that will help me create the success I desire?

1.

2.

3.

Thoughts/Insights/Feelings:

I Am Proud of Myself For….

Either YOU create the day or the day creates you....   Date _____

What is important to remember today (favorite scripture, quote, mantra, intention):

I Am_____   I Am_____

I Am_____   I Am_____

I Am_____   I Am_____

What I Am Grateful For:

What are the three (3) most important things I need to do today that will help me create the success I desire?

1.

2.

3.

Thoughts/Insights/Feelings:

I Am Proud of Myself For….

Either YOU create the day or the day creates you....   Date _____

What is important to remember today (favorite scripture, quote, mantra, intention):

I Am_____   I Am_____

I Am_____   I Am_____

I Am_____   I Am_____

What I Am Grateful For:

What are the three (3) most important things I need to do today that will help me create the success I desire?

1.

2.

3.

Thoughts/Insights/Feelings:

I Am Proud of Myself For....

Either YOU create the day or the day creates you….   Date _____

What is important to remember today (favorite scripture, quote, mantra, intention):

I Am_____   I Am_____

I Am_____   I Am_____

I Am_____   I Am_____

What I Am Grateful For:

What are the three (3) most important things I need to do today that will help me create the success I desire?

1.

2.

3.

Thoughts/Insights/Feelings:

I Am Proud of Myself For....

Successes and Celebrations

What am I most proud of? What did I accomplish these past few months?

What's my next level?

Made in USA - Kendallville, IN
15844_9781986941020
12.02.2021 1402